Everyday Magic

Everyday Magic

Poems and Selected Writings

Fancy Joy

First edition

ISBN: 979-8-218-85652-6

There are so many people I could dedicate this book to —
My loving husband, Randy, or my mom, Carolyn.
But this book is especially for Grammy Gertrude.
Her love of God and family lives on in me.
From her words I learned to listen,
From her heart, I learned to write.

Fancy Joy

Everyday life holds its own magic,
If we dare to see it.

Fancy Joy

Table of Contents

Introduction

Some of these words began as poems scribbled in a notebook, others as quick reflections posted online, and still others as thoughts that surfaced during quiet moments of everyday life. Together they form a kind of map — tracing where I've been, what I've learned, and the ways I've grown.

Everyday Magic: Poems and Selected Writings is a gathering of pieces from different seasons of my life, old and new, poem and prose. I chose to place them side by side because life itself rarely stays in neat categories; our moments of joy and sorrow, humor and reflection, wonder and routine all blend together. In the same way, the poems and prose here speak to one another, offering glimpses of the small miracles that appear when we pay attention.

This collection also includes several poems written by my beloved Grammy Gertrude — treasures from the "Grammy Book." Her words shaped me as a writer and as a person, and it is an honor to share them alongside my own.

My hope is that as you read these words, you'll feel a connection — to a memory, a feeling, or a spark of your own everyday magic. May this collection be an invitation to pause, to notice, and to discover beauty, hope, and light in the spaces between the ordinary.

Thank you for letting me share this journey with you.

Grammy Gertrude

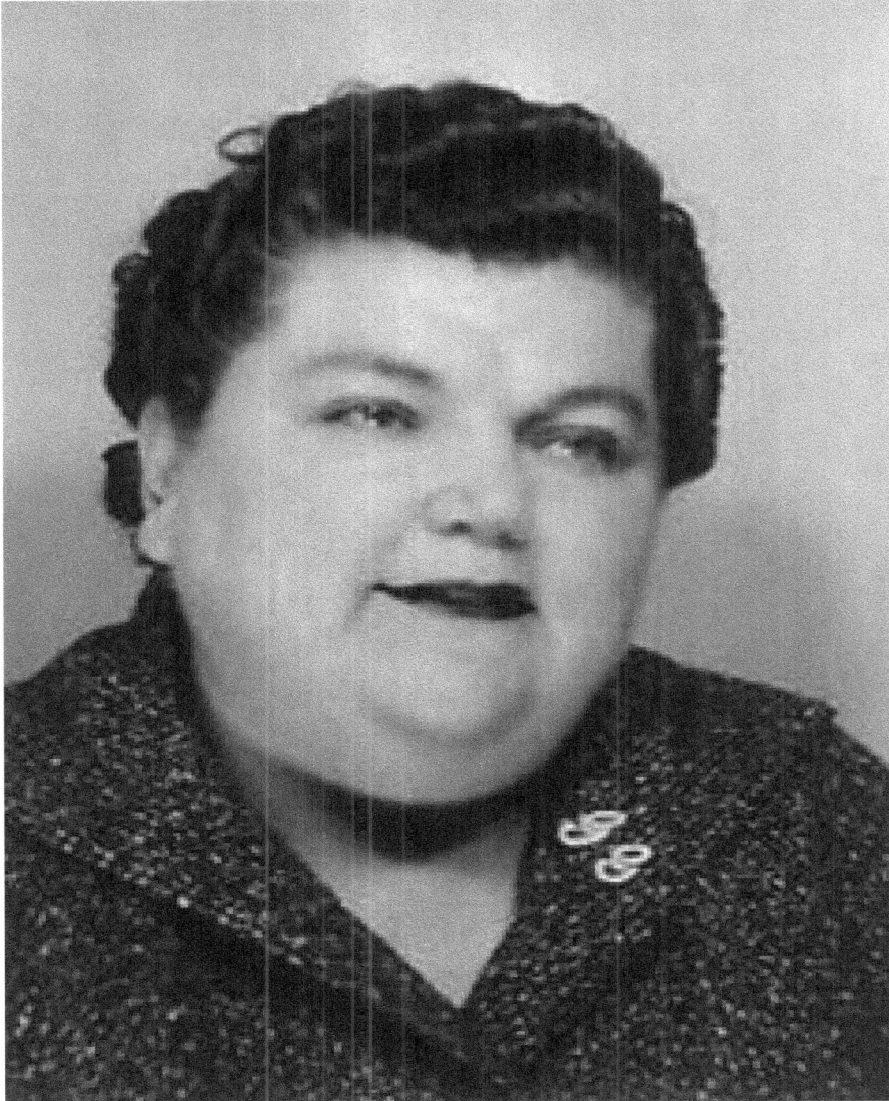

My Name Is Fancy Joy

I'd like to introduce myself to you
My name is Fancy Joy, but I've been blue
I've been through some life changes that were rough
God helped me make it through, but it was tough

I got married when I was twenty-two
At twenty-eight I had my son Andrew
I read to him every night before bed
Dr. Seuss got rhyming stuck in my head

I was married to Jim for thirty years
When he got cancer, we had to switch gears
He was bed bound and couldn't be alone
For a year I took care of him at home

After he died, I lost my sense of self
I even put my heart up on the shelf
To gather dust and not get hurt again
I'd be the lonely widow 'til the end

But God had already worked it all out
Now I'm so happy that I want to shout
An old flame found me on Facebook and now
I married my best friend and soul mate, wow!

Randy and I are good for each other
We love and understand one another
Respect and encouragement help us both
To flourish and maintain personal growth

I want others going through Life Changes
To not give up hope, life goes in stages
Be patient, things will turn around again
Good times will return, we just don't know when

Thanks for reading all the way to the end
Follow me on Facebook, I'll be your friend
I offer encouraging words that rhyme
Well, maybe they don't rhyme all of the time.

Here I am at my desk in what we call "The Captain's Quarters".

Anniversary Poem

It was thirty-six years ago today
We stood at the altar, and we did say
Vows that included 'til death do us part
But I didn't think that you would depart

We had thirty years together before
Cancer took you away from me and more
It took away my laughter and my fun
I couldn't be consoled by anyone

I didn't even take care myself
Thank God for our son, he was a big help
Even more than he was in your last days
He's a lot like you in so many ways

My grief was compounded by other things
People kept dying, our dog got her wings
I lost my job and had to sell our home
Got rid of too much stuff to move back home

Just when things seemed to be settling down
That's when the pandemic came into town
More people died, and I just couldn't cope
I felt I was at the end of my rope

But God had other plans for me, it's true
With therapy I stopped feeling so blue
I picked myself up and got through my grief
I felt much better, it's beyond belief

That's when I started dating someone new
And I really hope it's okay with you
That I married him and became his wife
But from what I'm told you know of this life

When you were here you could take care of me
And I wouldn't put it past you to see
That someone else would come into my life
To take care of me and make me his wife

You are still watching over us, I know
And you can hear what we say, and so
I thank you from the bottom of my heart
For our years together and now apart.

Our wedding photo.

Our last vacation together.

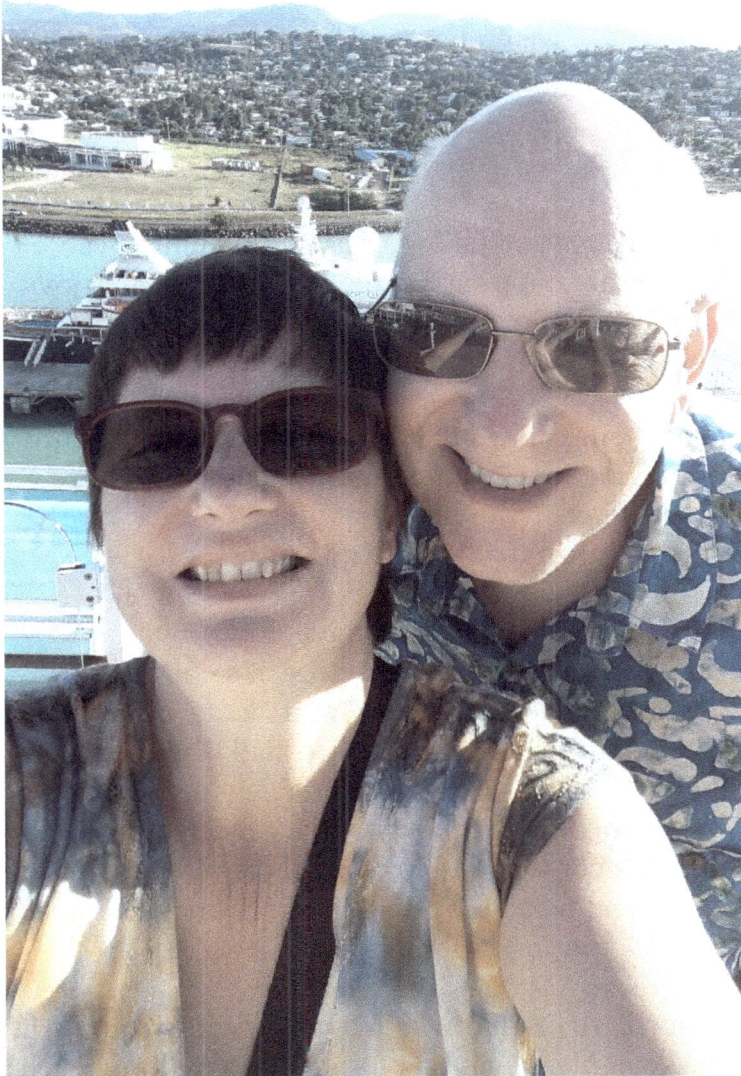

Birthday Remembrances

Today was my birthday which started me thinking
How I got this darn old I haven't an inkling
I reminisced of days when my worries were small
There were some days when I had no worries at all

The carefree days of taking naps and playing toys
Back when my happiness came from life's simple joys
Like mom really loving the coloring I did
or going out to play with a neighborhood kid

There are some things that I really miss that's for sure
While playing toys and taking naps has some allure
There are things that I miss that you wouldn't expect
One of the things that I really miss is respect

Do unto others as you would have done to you
I'm sure you have heard this before, it's nothing new
Say "Please" and "Thank You" and "Excuse Me" when you sneeze
Once you start doing it I think you will be pleased

In all you do, do more than what is expected
It will help everyone feel loved and respected
Be honest and true with all your words and your deeds
Have consideration for other people's needs

"Ask, don't tell" is about showing respect with speech
"Would you please get that for me it's out of my reach?"
I say that a lot 'cause I'm vertically challenged
Now I'm really stuck, what rhymes with challenged?

I feel like people have forgotten these lessons
The "norm" these days are "acceptable" transgressions
I hope this poem will help you to remember
The lessons you learned when you were young and tender

I was about two years old.
I look like I was up to something!

Just Another Day

To you it might be just another day
with early autumn colors on display
Everything's busy, kids are back in school
Dress in layers, the air is crisp and cool

But for me it won't ever be mundane
'Least not within the conforms of my brain
Because my life changed so much on that day
My husband died and my whole world turned gray

Of course, I think of him on other days
But "special days" are different in some ways
Birthdays, wedding days and death days are hard
Those days for me will forever be scarred

If you've lost someone you know what I mean
Keep yourself busy, thankful for routine
All day long you are stuck inside your head
Want to turn right, but you turn left instead

So, if you see someone struggling today
You never know if it's a "special day"
So please be nice and give them a warm smile
It may be the first they've seen in a while.

Jim and our son Andrew.

Inside Outside

You see that woman over there?
The one with all the bright red hair
and tattooed from her head to toes
with earrings in her face and nose

You might look at her with disgust
as if she's someone you can't trust
because she chose to look that way
you won't give her the time of day

You have no clue what she is like
underneath all those big red spikes
She may be someone sweet as pie
Or someone trying not to cry

You don't know all that she's been through
Her mother died when she was two
Her dad, he tried, but he was sad
and always seemed to be real mad

He drank too much and left her too
When she was only twenty-two
She had to make it on her own
That's when she moved in with Tyrone

He took good care of her at first
But then it started getting worse
He'd beat her up and tear her down
She always seemed to wear a frown

Until one day she had enough
Was through with life being so rough
She gathered all her strength and might
and left him on that very night

She had been homeless for awhile
Until the day that she met Kyle
He helped her to get off the street
Made sure she had enough to eat

He treated her with great respect
Which helped her gain her self-respect
They found the one that they had sought
They fell in love and tied the knot

They run a homeless shelter now
it's on a farm, they have a cow
They help others who are in need
I know that somehow, they'll succeed

I hope this story helps you see
That everyone's like you and me
Don't judge people by their outside
What matters is on the inside

Grammy Gertrude's book.

Don't judge a book by its cover!
There are so many precious things in this book.

A Little Boy's Nightmare

I was never so scared in all my life
As I was the other night,
It's a mighty good thing that I'm here now
'Cause I almost died from fright.

It was not yet dark when I got sent to bed,
To decide if obedient I'd be,
How could I be good when I had fun being bad?
Oh Golly, Oh Gosh, Oh Gee.

Stubbornly I stamped to bed about eight,
And pretended I was sleeping at nine,
As I lay there, I thought of how naughty I'd been,
Was it better to obey and be kind?

I was sorry, a little, but then I had fun,
Picking fights with the boy next door,
'N I blacked his eyes, 'cause he ain't so tough,
Then I punched him and teased him some more.

At dinner I spilled my glass of milk
Gulped soup and chewed aloud,
But worse than all that I had started to eat,
while the others' heads were still bowed.

I had squeezed the cat and pulled her tail,
and made her cry Meow.
'N I swiped some fruit from the corner store,
Which brought lines to Daddy's brow.

With my eyes tight closed, I waited for sleep -
but my thoughts were a million miles far,
The moon came up and frowned on me,
And so did each twinkling star.

I was weary and tired when sleep came at last
In a dream - on a carpet I flew,
Through meadows, o'er bridges and over the trees,
The sky was a sea of deep blue.

Then suddenly every noise was still,
I knew goblins were somewhere near,
'cause the goose bumps crept along my skin,
How I wished for my mommy dear?

But I couldn't walk, nor could I run,
Though I tried, believe you me.
When an eerie voice laughed HO, HO, HO,
I cried "Please let me be."

He was dressed in red and carried a stick,
and his eyes flashed green and gold.
And though it was summer when I had gone to sleep
I shivered because I was cold.

I reached for the covers, and rolled around
and fell to the floor with a clatter,
I called for Mommy and Daddy came too
"Oh son", they asked "What is the matter?"

Now warmly enclosed in Dad's loving arms,
And Mom's soothing words in my ears,
With the boogie-man far off in the land of my dream,
There's nothing to scare me so hear – that

I'm sorry, a lot, and I'm sure I can have fun,
being the best I know how to be.
If I tried to be good, I'm sure that I could,
Now just you wait and see.

Written by Grammy Gertrude in 1948

I was trying to be creative while taking this picture of the moon.
You should have seen me trying to get into just the right position!

Who Cares What Vehicle Your Soul Is In

Last night I was half asleep and half awake and I was dreaming about being interviewed on TV. I was explaining my philosophy about how we all tend to describe people based on physical traits. "That Jewish guy" or "The woman with the weird eyes" or "The gay kid at the grocery store". We even do in our heads when we are thinking of someone.

We should not describe each other by what the person physically looks like. We should not describe someone as a black woman. We should describe her as a well-liked, compassionate businesswoman who shares herself and her success with other people. We should not describe someone as an LGBTQ person. We should say they are sweet, honest, and they are easy to talk to.

We should not describe someone by their limitations either. It's not a man in a wheelchair; it's a very intelligent and humorous man who would give you the shirt off his back.

Do you get what I'm saying? Who cares about the vehicle your soul is in! Who cares what color it is or if it's all banged up. It's your soul that makes you different. Not your body. Not your religion. Not your clothing, not your piercings or tattoos (or lack thereof). It's your spirit, your soul, your energy. There are other people with the same skin tone as you. There are other people who follow the same religion as you. But you, your energy, your spirit and your soul are unique. There is not one other person out there who is exactly like you, not one other person who has had the exact same life experiences as you. You are a unique and beautiful soul.

We need to train ourselves to change the way we think about people. Change the way we describe people to ourselves and to each other.

And, when we find the wonderful uniqueness in someone, we should TELL THEM! Let others know what you see in them that is so beautiful and wonderful. Think of how you would feel if someone said to you, "You have a wonderful way of making people feel heard." or "You really light up a room with happiness when you walk in."

Give it a try. It takes some effort, but it's worth it! You could start by doing it for one person each day. What is something unique and/or wonderful about their soul?

Try it; you'll like it! And some day someone will tell YOU about YOUR wonderful, beautiful uniqueness.

I love taking pictures of nature.
Do you think this bird has a soul? I do.

Family Feuds

I know quite a few people who have family feuds. I really don't understand how people can let them continue. Family is family. People are people.

How do some people continue to not speak to certain members of their own family? Little disagreements have been blasted way out of proportion. They have gone on for years or even decades! Everyone makes mistakes. Everyone has feelings. Get over it and move on! They are your family. Forgive and forget. Agree to disagree. If more people would treat each other with respect, empathy, and love, this wouldn't happen.

I know I've forgiven people for things they have said or done. It may have taken a little while, but eventually I got over it and forgave them (and/or myself). People are precious. People are all we have! Friends and Family is what life is all about. Not things, not places. Not money, not objects. People. If you've lost a loved one, you know this! People are irreplaceable and time is precious.

It's like in my *Rose Colored Glasses* poem published in my book *Life Changes*. We are all the same at the core!

> You think I see people through rose colored glasses
> See only the good in everyone who passes
> But I do see the things other people call flaws
> I understand them so they don't cause me to pause
>
> When dealing with people I try to remember
> That we're all the same, so I don't lose my temper
> We are humans and perfection can't be achieved
> It really comes down to how these things are perceived
>
> Every person in this world has made some mistakes
> Everyone has feelings and have suffered heartaches
> We all have parts of our past we want to forget
> We have all said and done some things that we regret

We all want to feel we are heard and respected
The caring and kindness we show be reflected
Each one of us have our own beliefs, dreams and fears
There've been times in our lives that have brought us to tears

People are just people, we all want the same things
To be loved by each other without any strings
To feel like we matter, our lives make a difference
To know that there's a reason for our existence

True happiness is what we are all striving for
Do you see how we are all the same at the core?
So put on your own pair of rose colored glasses
And see all the good in everyone who passes

Lady bugs always remind me of my dad.

Bad Drivers

Today on the road I said something mean
To a man driving a car that was green
I said it out loud as if he could hear
And motioned with my hand, it was severe

Then I said out loud "what is your problem?"
That made me think, I don't know his problems
Maybe he's late for a job interview
I really don't know what he's going through

Was there a reason he did what he did?
What was the cause of him "flipping his lid"?
How was he feeling, was he really stressed?
Was he angry, hurt, or was he depressed?

Was someone else mean to him this morning?
Did he get bad news? Is he in mourning?
Did he just learn that his wife has cancer?
Did he propose and get the wrong answer?

Is he late for picking up his young kids
Did his father fall and injure his ribs?
Was his sister taken to the ER?
Did his long lost aunt return from afar?

Then I realized what I have to do
Change my reaction, change my point of view
From now on when drivers make me upset
I'll make up a story, as if we met!

That woman who is driving awfully slow
Was in a car accident years ago
She was driving too fast and lost control
The accident killed her best friend Nicole

It took her years to be able to drive
But that's why she only goes fifty-five
Although the speed limit is higher here
She's afraid to go faster, the poor dear

I think it's important to realize
Being angry at others is unwise
It doesn't hurt them, it just hurts ourselves
We can't change them, but we can change ourselves.

How amazing are butterflies!
This one is my favorite color, yellow.

Freedom of Speech

Sometimes one person thinks one way
And someone else thinks another
They both have the freedom to say
What they're thinking to the other

It's okay to have a debate
Free speech should not be neglected
But it's not okay to spread hate
Everyone should be respected.

Fireworks over the water are even more spectacular.

We're All Apples

People and apples are alike
There may be some that you don't like
There are many different colors
Some are sweet and some are sour

Some are real and some may be fake
Some are growing near The Great Lakes
There are different sizes and shapes
Some are only good when half-baked

No matter how they are different
I think they're all magnificent
I hope that we can all agree
They're all still apples, do you see?

We're all apples!

We like to go crabbing in the Indian River Bay in Delaware.

The Cardinal

I saw a red cardinal in a tree,
Did he come by just to visit with me?
Is he the spirit of a loved one lost?
Who is it sitting out there in the frost?

I wanted to take a picture of him
Sitting there pretty, perched high on that limb
The white of the snow against the brown bark
His bright crimson color really was stark

But before I could get him in focus
He disappointed this here poetess
By flying away and out of my sight
At least he gave me this poem to write!

Could this be the same cardinal?

Tall Trees

Tall Trees standing naked in the cold wind
Waiting patiently for the winter to end
Even though the winter seems oh so long
They know that soon they will hear the bird's song.

The view that inspired the poem.

The Seasons

Outside the soft white snow is falling,
Drifting and piling against the fence,
The sky is gray
The Trees are bare
A winter wonderland everywhere.

Once grew those fields with deep green grass
un-mown by the servant's hand,
And joyfully tossed
In the summer breeze,
Lies still in the winter's seize.

I do not know what I would do
Without the blossoms of spring
Or the summer warmth
And the autumn's fruit,
And the beauty the winter brings.

By Grammy Gertrude

The snow piling against the fence in our yard.

Orion's Belt

Whenever I am outside in the dark
There is a search on which I will embark
I scan, I squint, and I turn all around
I'm seeing if my old friend can be found

I only know a few constellations
and I'm never sure of their locations
But Orion's Belt seems easy to find
The three stars that are so neatly aligned

I know it may seem weird to you at first
But he was there when life was at its worst
Things were changing and the future was blurred
I couldn't bare everything that occurred

I was so scared, and I felt all alone
It was unlike anything I had known
Nothing was right and life felt so unfair
But I looked at the sky, and he was there

It was comforting that he stayed the same
when everything else was going insane
I felt like he grounded me at a time
when out of my skin I wanted to climb

He helped to calm me when nothing else could
Everything will work out, all will be good
I wasn't alone, someone else was there
Someone to turn to when life seemed unfair

It was much later that I came to see
It was really God who was there for me
He used Orion's Belt as a proxy
Because it was something that I could see

Now when I see those three stars in the sky
I feel like it's really God saying "Hi"
I am here for you, don't be despondent
My love for you is forever constant

See the belt in the middle? The three stars so neatly aligned.

Early Morning Magic

In the early morning magic hour, when the light from the sun is barely peeking over the horizon, and the trees are black silhouettes against the barely lit golden blue sky, a multitude of birds simultaneously sing out their chirps, tweets and whistles, creating a joyful symphony as if proclaiming the night is over, all is well, and a brand-new day has begun. Even the owl chimes in as if saying "My watch is done, you take the day".

Such a beautiful moment.

Can you hear the symphony in your mind?

Water

Just what is it about water
that makes us feel so very good
Is exactly what I pondered
while in the hot shower I stood

Whether shower or bath we take
We don't ever want to get out
Is it the ocean or the lake?
Do you fish for flounder or trout?

If we're not in it or on it
For whatever is the reason
Then we'll settle to be near it
It doesn't matter the season

We long to experience it
with any of our five senses
Hear it, see it, smell it, taste it
Feeling it eases our stresses

To sit and listen to the waves
Or hear the babble of a stream
I think that's what my body craves
So I no longer want to scream

The rumble of a waterfall
As it tumbles down the mountain
Is more exciting after all
Than the trickle of a fountain

To see all of the greens and blues
as they mix and swirl together
There are so many different hues
depending upon the weather

To gaze upon a shiny lake
or be mesmerized by the sea
Is what I want, make no mistake
That is the perfect place for me

How soothing is that first big sniff
of the salty ocean breezes
or when your mom gets her first whiff
of the pool and then she sneezes

Some people say it has no taste
But I really beg to differ
It depends on if you are placed
Near an ocean or a river

I think that we can all agree
That we really love the water
It would be really great if we
Thanked God for giving us water.

Ah, the ocean. My body instantly relaxes at the thought of being there.

Do you see the rainbow?

Stop and Smell the Flowers

Most likely we have all heard this at some point. But did you ever stop to think what it really means?

To me, it means this:

> We should all, every day, take some time, even just a minute or two, to stop what we are doing and pause.
>
> Take some time to look around at this beautiful world. Take a moment to really listen to the birds singing.
>
> Truly examine the flowers, the trees, the squirrels, the chipmunks. Watch a bee going from one flower to another.
>
> Stop and smile at some children playing, or a couple walking hand in hand.
>
> Look at the sky, the sun, the clouds, the moon, the stars.
>
> Enjoy the beauty that surrounds us and the miracles that God gave us.
>
> Be in the moment.
>
> Take some time to enjoy life.
>
> This gives us the chance to slow ourselves down, relax, and breathe.
>
> Stop your brain from thinking too much. Give yourself a break.
>
> Rejuvenate your body, mind, spirit, and soul.

All flowers are beautiful, even if they don't have a strong aroma.
All people are beautiful, even if they try to hide it.

Our Minds

Today I had a memory
of a place I lived as a child
It was so very sensory
That I closed my eyes and I smiled

I could picture every detail
and I thought I could smell it too
So I took a great big inhale
which really sharpened up the view

I almost heard the sounds I'd hear
When I was in that tiny room
I wanted to make them more clear
There were more details to exhume

Our minds can be so powerful
If we would only let them try
The gifts they have are bountiful
If we don't let them go awry

With a little concentration
We can travel through time and space
Can visit any location
And even see anyone's face

If you're in a situation
Or if everything feels hectic
Just use your imagination
and visit somewhere exotic

Or if you really miss someone
who has gone to a better place
Close your eyes and you can summon
a vivid picture of their face

And if you listen carefully
You can probably hear them talk
They're saying very fervently
Beside you they will always walk

Sisters on Christmas morning. I loved that doll house.

One Less Splinter

My mother often took me to visit my grandmother when I was a child. She lived in a small row home in Allentown, PA. I remember her teeny tiny backyard very fondly. She had some grass with a cement sidewalk splitting it into two small strips. Just outside the grass on either side, right next to the fences, she had her flower beds. They were always filled with beautiful, fragrant flowers. Her favorite flowers were "Blue Flags" as we called them (even though they weren't all blue). I know now that they were Irises. I remember enjoying their colors and fragrances but always being on the lookout for bees!

Anyway, on this particular sunny day I decided to run up and down the "ramp" created by the outside doors that led to her basement. They were old and the wood was all splintered. My mother told me to stop playing on those doors, but of course I didn't heed her warnings. I fell and slid palms down on the splintered wood which filled both of my tiny hands with little fragments of wood. My parents spent hours with tweezers and a needle, removing them one at a time.

There are so many things in life that "drive us crazy" that are out of our control. Sometimes we can feel overwhelmed and/or feel like we have no control over what is happening. A bunch of little things can make that one last thing seem so big (the straw that broke the camel's back). When in actuality, it's just one more little thing. Maybe we should concentrate on changing the things that we can control. If we do this, if we can alleviate little stressors, it can help us to feel more "in control" of our lives.

Every time you find yourself saying "this drives me crazy", do something about it. Take the time to change something or fix something.

For example: Every time I put clean towels out in the bathroom, it annoyed me that I had to unfold the towels and fold them again to put them on the towel rack.

Let me explain. Our bath towels are large and two won't fit next to each other on the towel rack unless they are folded in thirds. When we do laundry, we fold the towels in half (old habits I guess).

So, every time I changed the towels in the bathroom, I had to unfold them and refold them into thirds before I could hang them on the rack. It's little, I know! But every time I did it, it bothered me. Until finally I said to myself, Fancy, what are you doing? Why don't you just fold them in thirds right away when you take them out of the dryer? (DUH!)

And now that I do that, when I put clean towels out in the bathroom I smile instead of frown. You'll be surprised at how that one little thing makes a difference. It's one less splinter!

Me and Grammy Gertrude in her backyard. I remember her dog, Pepe.

Do Something Different

Do one thing that is new today
Do something different in some way
Add something special to your home
Add some excitement of your own

It could be something oh so small
Hang a new picture on the wall
Listen to music you don't know
Go someplace you don't always go

Change one little thing, it's not hard
Go outside and sit in the yard
Turn off your phone and read a book
Or style your hair for a new look

Sometimes we feel like we are stuck
In a rut that makes us say YUK
But if we do just one thing new
It helps to change our point of view

My Aunt Dee made this picture for me.
It hangs in our bathroom above the towels that are folded in thirds.

Be The Dream

Don't think of yourself as small
Don't look at yourself at all
Concentrate on the dream-you
And watch as your dream comes true

Be the dream!

These baby robins hatched in a bush next to our house.

Here And Now

Sometimes it's easy to get caught up in the past
Traumas we have endured have caused scars that will last
Memories of lost loved ones can make us somber
Not to mention all the What If's that we ponder

Sometimes we reminisce about times we had fun
All the smiles and laughter we shared with our loved ones
We should be happy we had those times together
But somehow it makes us miss them more than ever

Sometimes we worry too much about tomorrow.
So focused that it makes our thinking too narrow
Maybe this and maybe that, what if, and then how?
Our brain is too busy to enjoy what is now

Sometimes we will need to help ourselves get unstuck
I'll share a little trick that has brought me some luck
The past or the future, if your brain's stuck in these
You just say to yourself "Here and Now if you please"

Don't dwell in the past or fret about tomorrow
It won't change anything and will bring you sorrow
Sometimes we can think about these things, It's Okay
As long as we don't forget to enjoy today.

I call these birds "Long Neckers".

This guy is hanging out at the "Turtle Pond".

Wash The Day Away

I don't remember where I heard it, or if it's even true, but it took hold in my brain, and I am thankful.

Police officers can see a lot of bad things during their day. So, at the end of their shift, when they take off their uniform, they consciously leave the day with their uniform. When they put the uniform in their locker, they leave the job with it, so they don't take it home with them.

I transformed it into something that I could do.

At night, when I wash my face to get ready for bed, I wash the day off. I consciously think to myself as I am washing my face that I am washing the day off. It's done, it's over, I can't change it. Wash it off and be done with it. Tomorrow is another day.

Even now, when I've had a great day, there is going to be something in my brain that is bothering me. I let it go down the drain, and I think about how great the day was and how tomorrow can be even better.

I've taken a number of pictures of the moon in my day.

This is one of the best.

God Works In Mysterious Ways

Sometimes things happen in just the right way
We are amazed at the complex array
Of things that fell into just the right place
How terrible if that wasn't the case

"It was perfect timing" someone may say
It couldn't have worked any other way
God works in mysterious ways, It's true
He's worked it all out, for me and for you.

Timing is everything.

Photographs Of Times Gone Past

Looking at photographs of times gone past
Those were the days we thought would always last
But time does go by and many things changed
Our entire lives have been re-arranged

If we could visit ourselves on that day
Talk to ourselves, what on earth would we say?
Would we warn ourselves of future mistakes?
Say "Please don't do that, whatever it takes!"

Do we warn of loved ones' impending deaths?
Tell us to enjoy each and every breath
Would we offer words of encouragement?
Say "All your dreams are within attainment"?

Would we inform ourselves what stock to buy?
To be sure that money's in high supply
Do we try to stop future disasters?
Or delve into political matters?

Would you tell yourself "It'll be okay!
Everything supposed to happen that way
You may feel like things are going all wrong
But things will turn around, it won't take long"

We need the hard times to make us stronger
Learn from our mistakes, our fears to conquer
We wouldn't be just who we are today
If it wasn't for what happened yesterday

Me and my son Andrew on vacation at the beach.

Do you have any keyhole keepsake pictures?

Baby Carolyn

From the Grammy Gertrude book. In the book it says my mom was ten months old when Grammy wrote this poem about her.

Her eyes are dark, her cheeks are pink,
Her hair is golden brown,
Those chubby legs and dimpled hands,
Sure scatter toys around.

With a great big smile and a whispered "Da",
she coaxes Daddy to play,
With rattles and balls and blocks and dolls
That make up a baby's day.

She puts her little hand in his,
Two feet prance on the floor,
And stepping lightly here and there,
The big room they explore.

Having seen her brothers with trucks and cars,
Crawl over the big brown chair,
She'd like to make the cars move too,
But the roads just aren't there.

And there's the phone, she's heard the ring,
Then someone says Hello,
So Daddy lets her listen to
Grammy's voice so soft and low.

Next is the shelf where magazines,
Are piled in twos and threes,
Chock full of pictures and, Oh such
Cute babies there, you'll see.

Around the room they walk again,
It was very nice to be
Outside the play-yard where it's safe,
For such little ones as she.

Now tired and sleepy,
She's on the way,
On a journey that ends
With another day

By Grammy Gertrude

Aunt Marilyn holding my ten-month-old mom.

Although

Although it's overcast and the sky is all gray
The air still smells salty, and sea gulls still play
Although the sun isn't shining warm on my skin
It isn't yet raining and I'm outside, not in

Although it was only a short ride on the bay
It still gave me the peace that's been running a-stray
Although I couldn't seem to put my mind at ease
I got it to focus and write poems that please

Although summer is coming down to the wire
We'll soon be enjoying the warmth of the fire
Although the sun is setting earlier each day
It gives us more time to enjoy the stars that way

Although you see something as being negative
You can train yourself to find something positive
Although it'll be hard the first time you do it
Keep on trying and soon you'll get the hang of it

Sometimes things don't go just the way we expected
Wouldn't it be great if we learned to accept it
The sun is always shining behind the gray skies
Just look for the "Although's" it'll open your eyes

While sailing on the Indian River Bay in Delaware,
I captured this picture and this poem.

Christmas Ornaments

Hanging ornaments on the Christmas tree
Is a very special project to me
It's something that I take seriously
I perform it oh so reverently

Not only do I strive for perfection
in their placement and in their direction
Their size also determines where they go
Big ones up high is a real no-no

Don't put two red ones next to each other
You've got to try to spread out the color
If it's stained glass be sure the light shines through
It really helps with the overall view

But that is not the most important part
It's what I feel way down deep in my heart
For I have attained quite a collection
of ornaments that cause some reflection

I have some that were hanging on the tree
in my childhood house when I was just three
I have some made by my son in preschool
One is a cut-out of his hand, how cool!

Some remind me of loved ones who have died
Forever in my heart they will reside
The Eagles Football one is for my Dad
And the FedEx truck is for my son's Dad

Aunt Marilyn gave some cute ones to me
She dated them by hand, it's neat to see
I wish I had one for my Aunt Sandy
She really was my favorite Auntie

There's one in honor of each of my dogs
There's even one in the shape of a frog
It reminds me of my friends from Frog Town
There's also one that's the face of a clown

There are some from when my son was small
Every year I find a place for them all
I remember when he was a baby
I kind of miss those days, well maybe

There are even some in honor of me
Angel Daffy Duck is funny to see
A miniature mug with my name on it
A blue pedal car, I had one like it

There are some new ones that make me happy
A mini crab pot holding a crabbie
My soulmate's and my very first Christmas
The year we became Mr. & Mrs.

Each ornament is more than just a thing
I hold each one and the memory it brings
Remembering people and times gone by
It's okay if it sometimes makes me cry.

I am reverent with each and every one
I hope that I pass this on to my son
Take time to remember what's in the past
But always look forward, the future's vast.

This little ornament is a tracing of my young son's hand.

These hung on our tree when I was just three.

Christmas Joys

Little girl and little boy,
Come fill your hearts with Christmas Joy,
For long ago one star lit night,
The angels filled the sky so bright.

And told the shepherds where they lay,
That this would be a holy day.
For unto you a child is given
The hope of earth, the joy of Heaven.

Peace on earth, good will to men,
For Christ was born in Bethlehem.
Ah, there within a manger lay,
A savior, Christ, our Lord, today.

The perfect child, He made no sound
As shepherds and wise men gathered round,
To praise and worship, and to pray
A king was born that Christmas day.

by Grammy Gertrude

An angel ornament from my childhood.

Deja Vu

I think Deja Vu is God's way of telling you that you are exactly where you are meant to be, and everything is as it should be.

I used to be afraid of bees. Now I love taking pictures of them.

Such Beauty!

Seasons

You are my Winter.
You lit a fire in me to warm me
when I was cold, dark and stormy.

You are my Spring.
You put a spring in my step and my spirit.
You gave me new life.

You are my Summer.
You taught me that the sun is always behind
the clouds. You gave me fun and laughter.

You are my Autumn.
You put spice in my life. You reminded me
how colorful and beautiful life really is.

In a world of green, be orange.

More

Everything in life is more with you
I've never smiled so much in my life
More happiness than I ever knew
I'm so proud that I can be your wife

Everything in life is more with you
There is more kindness and more laughter
More music, more hugs and kisses too
It will always be more hereafter

I am happy that we're together
And I love you more than words can say
But I won't just love you forever
I'll love you forever and a day

Everything in life is more with you
I think what we have is more than love
And I know that you believe it's true
We both give thanks to our God above

Everything in life is more with you
I love you more each and every day
It's amazing how much our love grew
More than a hug and kiss can convey

I am happy that we're together
And I love you more than words can say
But I won't just love you forever
I'll love you forever and a day

We said "I Do".

See Clear

You tell me that I'm beautiful
I can tell you really mean it
You tell me that I'm talented
and you wish that I could see it

I tell you that you're wonderful
and I hope you know I mean it
I tell you that you're amazing
and I wish that you could see it

If only we could see ourselves
The same way we see each other
Then maybe we would love ourselves
The same way we love each other

But maybe that's why we are here
God put us together, my love
To help each other to see clear
That we are someone to be loved

Black-Eyed-Susans add sunshine to your life.

Holding Hands

What does it mean when we are holding hands?
I'll try my best to help you understand
That simple act is so complex, you see
It means so many different things to me

First of all, it always means I love you!
But it also means "I'm here for you" too
Together we'll face all the ups and downs
We will share everything from smiles to frowns

It also means I don't want to lose you
If there's a crowd of people to get through
Life's so much better when we're together
I want you to stay with me forever

Sometimes when I am feeling insecure
It's meant to show others you're mine for sure
There are times when I have anxiety
Your warm tender hand helps to quiet me

I want my hand to do the same for you
Provide comfort and security too
I hope whenever we hold hands it's clear
Together we both have nothing to fear

It's not just a habit or a routine
There are so many things that it can mean
What I've been trying to say from the start
When we hold hands, we hold each other's heart

Holding hands during our wedding ceremony.

But More Than That, You Are The One

You are my friend
but more than that
you are my best friend

You are my husband
but more than that
you are my partner

You are my happiness
but more than that
you are my love

You're the one that I rely on
the one that I can love on
My only heart's desire
You're all that I require
to have all my dreams come true
but more than that
you are The One

You are my confidante
but more than that
you are my confidence

You hold me up
but more than that
you build me up

You are my kindred spirit
but more than that
you are my Soul Mate

You're the one that I rely on
the one that I can love on
My only heart's desire
You're all that I require
to have all my dreams come true
but more than that
you are The One

He is the one.

Second Chance

We are so lucky, God gave us a second chance
We are not together because of happenstance
It all had to happen in exactly that way
I'm still your wife although there was a long delay

He gave us a second chance to be together
We each had separate storms that we had to weather
Our paths were meant to go in different directions
But we would always meet at this intersection

We have to live our lives for the here and the now
Dwelling on the past can only hurt us somehow
We can't be afraid of what the future may hold
We'll face it together however it unfolds

I am so grateful for everything that is us
Everything from the doldrums to the momentous
I'm even grateful for the years we were apart
They made us who we are today and shaped our hearts

So please don't feel bad for breaking up with me then
I know we keep saying it time and time again
Your brain knows all the facts we've discussed it before
Your heart should tell you that today I love you more

Two blooms on one stalk.
Me and Randy, two souls bound together with love.

I Love You

You should know that I love you
Because I say it every day
You can tell that I love you
by all the things I do and say

Still you ask why I love you
as if I could recite a list
I love you because you're you!
and it's you I cannot resist

My love for you will not fade
No matter what we may go through
There's no need to be afraid
of anything you say or do

I love you absolutely
I couldn't stop it if I tried
I love you so completely
every part and all of your sides

My love for you is constant
There's no start and it will not end
My love for you this instant
won't decrease, but it will transcend

Love grows.

Valentine

This Valentine's from me to you
Ah dream girl with your eyes so blue,
And smiling lips and golden hair,
Wish I were with you there.

As deep down as the deep blue sea,
Or high up as the sky,
I love you darlin', I always will,
Until the day I die.

I never can forget the day,
When I first held your hand,
And spelled the letters "I Love You",
A writing in the sand.

The sea has washed the words away,
But ever in my heart,
They're etched with tears and love, my dear
Though we are miles apart.

Pray tell me that you love me dear,
That you will wait for me,
That you are still my Valentine,
And I will happy be.

By Grammy Gertrude

The valentine Grammy Gertrude placed with her poem.

TO A DARN GOOD SKATE

MADE IN U. S. A.

It

I like it in the morning
And I want it around noon
I need it in the evening
Also when day is through

I like it after a meal
and when I'm really tired
It really is ideal
To make me feel inspired

I cannot go without it
No matter how hard I try
I really have to admit
It's a need I can't deny

There's nothing that can replace
All the things it does for me
You can see it on my face
How it gives me so much glee

I think about it all day
When can I have it again?
I want it without delay
Don't want to wait until "then"

You may be thinking "Come On"
What is this "It" you speak of
It's different for everyone
It is whatever you love

For me it is my husband
The one God made just for me
I want him to understand
Just how much he means to me

I hope you know that I pray
For you reading this right now
That there will soon be a day
Where you find your "it" somehow

When you see a rainbow, it is a sign of God's promise.

It's Hard To Type This

It's hard to type these words right now
But I will get it done somehow
They are ready to burst right out
If they stay, they will make me shout

I will do what I have to do
So that they don't come out askew
I hope that you can understand
That this was really so unplanned

There, that makes it so much better
I can quickly type each letter
It's like playing the Piana
Since I finished my banana!

This picture of the moon isn't perfect,
but it is perfectly unique.

Don't worry if you make a mistake,
you never know, it could turn out awesome!

April Fool's Day

April Fool's Day used to be lots of fun
I would try to pull a prank on someone
But not anymore, it's lost its appeal
It should be canceled, that's the way I feel

It's supposed to make us laugh and be fun
But it's done at the expense of someone
Making someone feel bad or like a fool
Or even get hurt, isn't really cool

So don't rig the sink to get someone wet
Don't text your mom that you got a new pet
Followed by a picture of a big snake
Or give dad a soda that you did shake

Don't call your aunt and tell her that you fell
You broke your leg and aren't feeling that well
Don't put vegetables in a doughnut box
Or fill the egg carton with some white rocks

When packing their lunch, don't send a raw egg
Don't tape a fake cockroach onto their leg
Or switch their sock and underwear drawers
Don't put "out of order" on all the doors

Whatever you do be careful today
There's just one more thing that I have to say
It shouldn't be a shock to anyone
April Fools! Please be safe but have some fun

Remember those baby robins?

Dutch Months

September- 'Specting Brrr
October – Aught to brrr
November – Now ve brr
December – Deese am brrr
January – Jan, You airy?
February – Yep, you airy?
March- Mar, chit's cold.
April – Ape, will it ever get warm?
May – Maybe dis month
June – Ju-know it's finally warm aut!
July – Ju-Lie it taint warm, it HOT
August – A-gust of wind be nice right 'bout now.

Drying its wings in the sun.

Nature is amazing!

Smart Billy

When you open up a can of food
and set it on the table,
The product never looks as good
as the picture on the label.

For garden truck could never glow
as brightly as the artists show.
But the goat is wiser than the man
He eats the label on the can.

This was written by my mother, Carolyn.

The first harvest from our back yard garden.

The Big Game

Today there will be a big football game
A team of players will obtain world fame
Everyone will be watching from somewhere
Even the ones who don't usually care

Because it's the biggest game of the year
Don't want to wait 'til tomorrow to hear
Which one of the teams will end up on top
Whatever you do don't interrupt pop

His team is playing this important game
He's yelling to all the players by name
As if they can hear him through the TV
If they would win, oh how happy he'd be

I'm just watching to see the commercials
I hope there's a good one using squirrels
I can't believe how much money is spent
To air thirty seconds in this event

I'd much rather watch the puppies at play
Aired on that animal channel today
I root for the team named RUFF in that game
There's just something I like about the name

Wherever you watch this big game today
There's just one more thing that I want to say
I don't want to make anybody cry
My Dad would want to say FLY EAGLES FLY!

I captured this great shot at my favorite zoo in Florida.

The Phone

Kids these days don't fully understand
Just what it is they hold in their hand
Things are so much easier for them
Not like it was for us way back when

Each home and business had just one phone
Pick it up and listen for the tone
Dialed the numbers to make a call
And then you were tethered to a wall

When the house phone rang we never knew
Who it was we would be talking to
We didn't know when a call was missed
Speaker phone didn't even exist

We all memorized the phone numbers
of our family, friends and the plumber
Or we looked them up in the phone book
If we knew exactly where to look

Our contacts list was made of paper
We used a pencil and eraser
When you were out and it was at home
There was no looking it up on Chrome

If the phone you called was being used
Then your call was so rudely refused
You'd hear the blaring busy signal
Which surely didn't make you giggle

There were times when you would be appalled
If no one answered the phone you called
You couldn't leave a message for them
Keep calling back until who knows when

There was no way to reach anyone
If they were outside having some fun
You couldn't text your mom or your dad
To tell them "We need milk real bad"

There was no such thing as GPS
We had to know how to go, or guess
Try to follow written directions
"Turn north at that weird intersection"

Don't even get me started about
the rest of the things we did without
social media, email and games
Instantly filing insurance claims

Not to mention all it required
To take pictures when you desired
A camera, film, a flash bulb and then
Can't see if it got 'til who knows when

Shopping was only done at a store
At times you went to three or to four
In order to get all that you need
But satisfaction was guaranteed!

Don't get me wrong, I love my cell phone
When it's with me, I'm never alone
But sometimes I long for way back when
All we needed was paper and pen

New Shoes

Why are new shoes comfortable in the store
Then you get home and they're not anymore

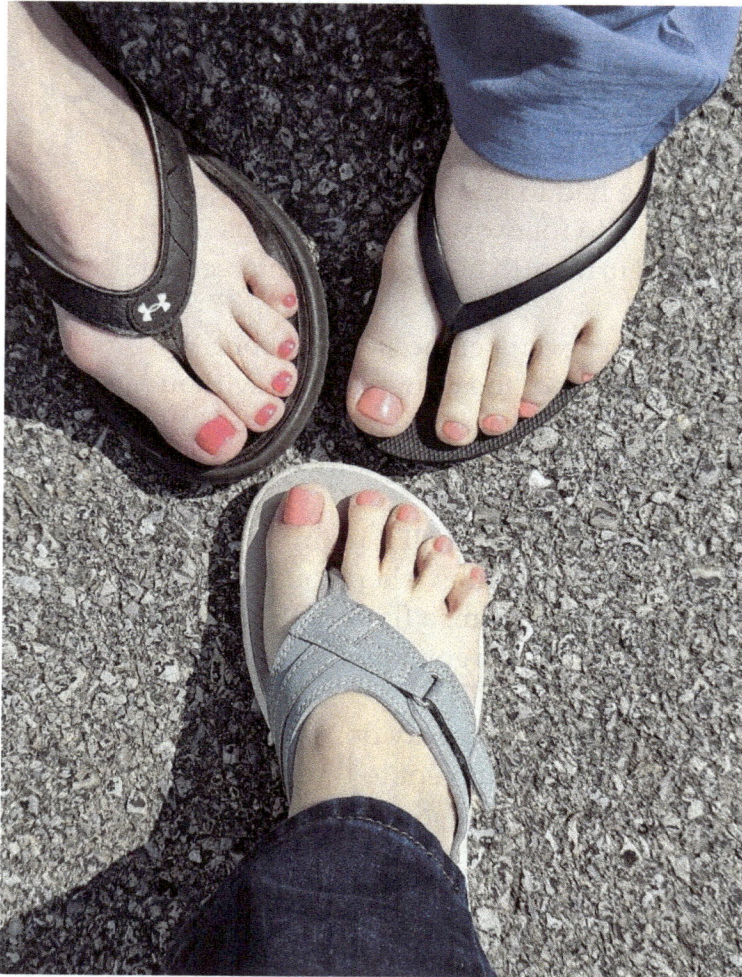

Of course I'm not talking about flip-flops.
I love this picture, taken when my sister, my niece and I got pedicures
on the first day of spring.

Ducks in the "Turtle Pond".

Practice

Practice, practice, and more practice
that's what the masters always say
In order to get good at this
you have to do it every day

I didn't have an idea
of what to write about today
Didn't know a panacea
or have a story to relay

Here I sit writing this poem
trying to do what I am told
I don't want it to be "ho-hum"
I want it to be solid gold

Sometimes it's hard to find the words
and then you have to make them rhyme
My brain says, "This is for the birds!"
Yet I come back, time after time

If at first it doesn't work out
maybe I have to step away
go for a little walk-about
I try to clear my head that way

So how much do I have to type
to make the practice count today
I hate to sound just like a gripe
but now I want to go and play

Sometimes my workspace is on the kitchen table.

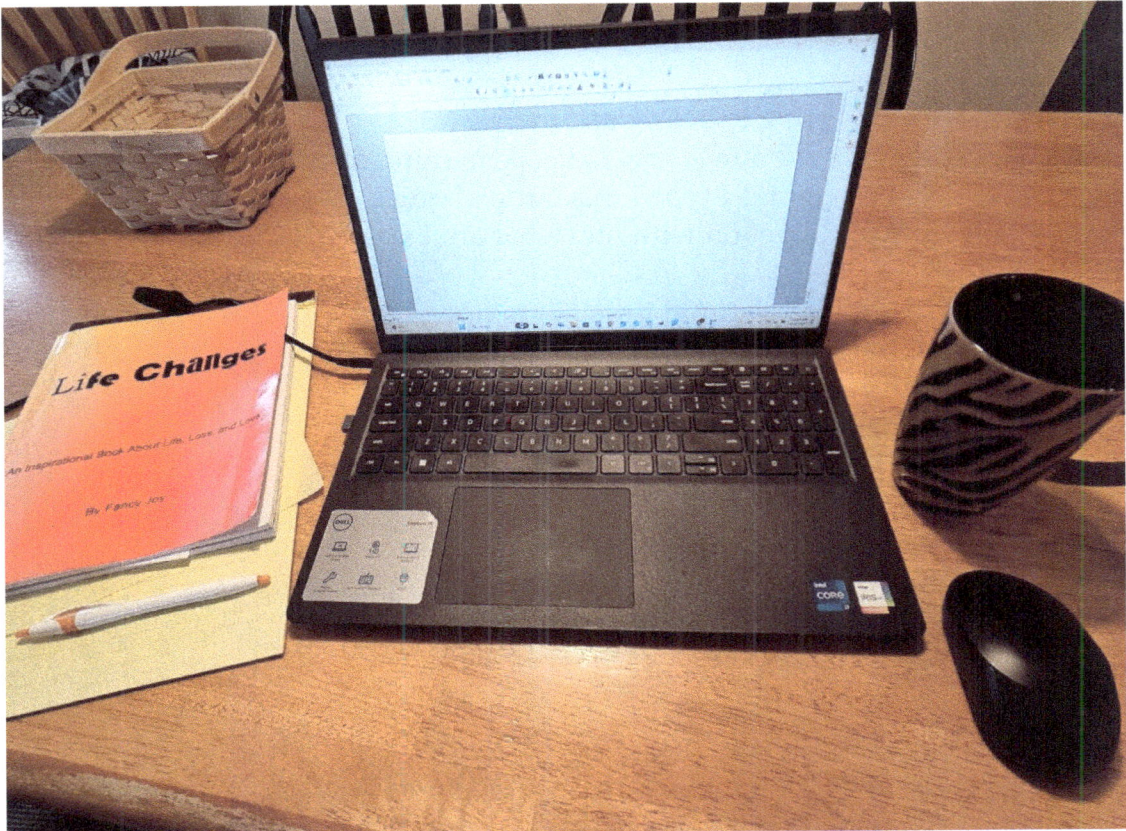

So Much To Say

There are so many things I want to say
But I have to pick only one each day
It took most of the day to write one poem
There's stuff to do, but my mind keeps going

I'm trying to get myself to the store
But my brain wants to keep rhyming some more
I thought if I typed this out real quick
I could get on with life, what am I sick?

It's such a stupid little poem now
But it just keeps on coming out somehow
Okay now I really have to move on
Before someone turns this into song

My sister's cat was sitting on the window behind a plant.
I love the way the green of the plant brings out the color of her eyes!

Thank You God

Have I thanked Thee, dear God,
For the love Thou has given,
To Thy children on earth
With the promise of Heaven.

Though this prayer be my thanks
May my deeds prove each day,
That I'm thankful, dear Lord,
Thou mayest have Thine own way.

Written by Grammy Gertrude.

Clouds and sky pictures are prevalent in my photo gallery.

About The Author

Fancy Joy is an inspirational writer with a passion for sharing stories of resilience, healing, and hope. Her debut book, Life Changes: An Inspirational Book about Life, Loss and Love, was written to encourage readers walking through seasons of transition, grief, and renewal.

With a heart for uplifting others, Fancy Joy blends honesty and compassion in her writing, reminding readers that even in life's hardest moments, there is always a spark of light to be found. When she isn't writing, she enjoys spending time with family, finding joy and magic in everyday moments, and encouraging others to keep moving forward with faith and courage.

Follow Fancy Joy for updates on her latest projects, book news, and encouragement for your own journey through life's changes.

Facebook: https://www.facebook.com/fancyjoyauthor
Instagram: @FancyJoyAuthor
You Tube: @FancyJoyAuthor
Web Site: https://fancyjoy0.wixsite.com/findjoy

Also By Fancy Joy

With an ocean of compassion and faith, Fancy Joy's writing guides readers through life's storms toward healing, hope, and renewed joy.

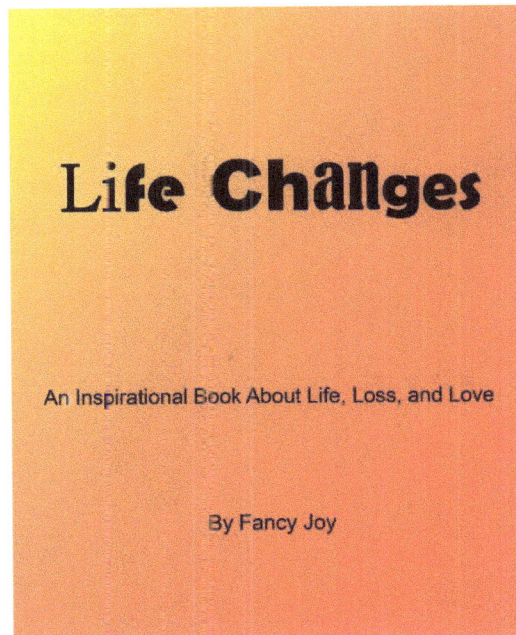

Life Changes: An Inspirational Book About Life, Loss, and Love

Life Changes is more than poetry — it's a journey through love, grief, faith, and the moments that shape us. With heartfelt poems and original photographs, this collection invites you to reflect, heal, and find inspiration in life's ups and downs.

www.ingramcontent.com/pod-product-compliance
Lightning Source LLC
Chambersburg PA
CBHW081156270326
41930CB00014B/3174